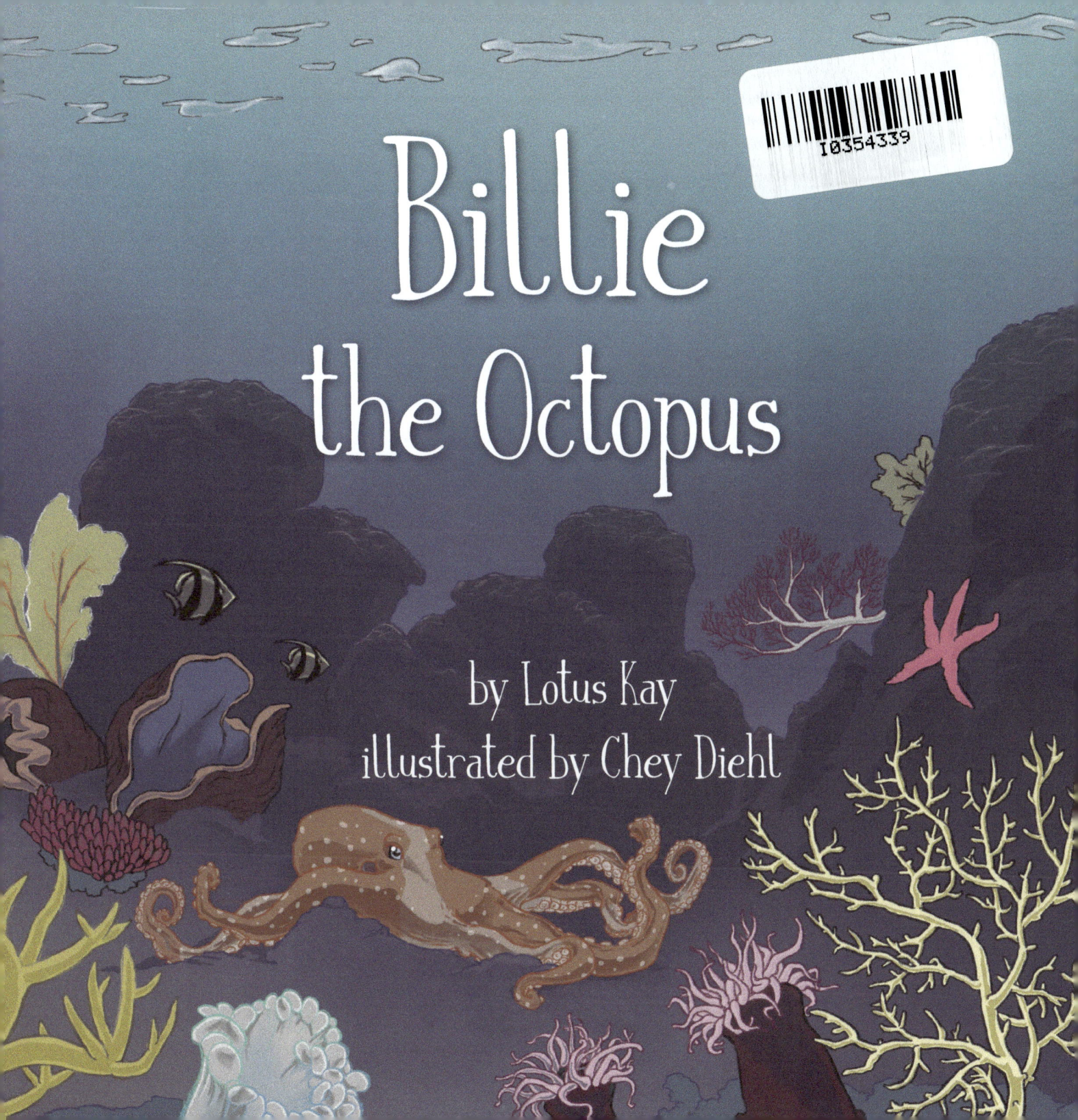

At Eifrig Publishing, our motto is our mission —
"Good for our kids, good for our Earth, and good for our communities."
We are passionate about helping kids develop into caring, creative, thoughtful individuals who possess positive self-images, celebrate differences, and practice inclusion. Our books promote social and environmental consciousness and empower children as they grow in their communities.
www.eifrigpublishing.com

© 2019 Lotus Kay

Printed in the United States of America

All rights reserved. This publication is protected by Copyright, and permission should be obtained from the publisher prior to any prohibited reproduction, storage in a retrieval system, or transmission in any form or by any means, electronic, mechanical, photocopying, recording, or likewise.

Published by Eifrig Publishing,
PO Box 66, Lemont, PA 16851, USA
Knobelsdorffstr. 44, 14059 Berlin, Germany.

For information regarding permission, write to:
Rights and Permissions Department,
Eifrig Publishing, PO Box 66, Lemont, PA 16851, USA.
permissions@eifrigpublishing.com, +1-888-340-6543

Library of Congress Cataloging-in-Publication Data

Kay, Lotus
Billie the Octopus/
by Lotus Kay, illustrated by Chey Diehl
p. cm.

Paperback: ISBN 978-1-63233-236-3
Hard cover :ISBN 978-1-63233-231-8
Ebook: ISBN 978-1-63233-232-5

[1.Environment - Juvenile Fiction. 2. Conservation - Juvenile Fiction 3. Earth Day - Juvenile Fiction]

I. Chey Diehl , ill. II. Title

23 22 21 20 2019
5 4 3 2 1

Printed on recycled acid-free paper. ∞

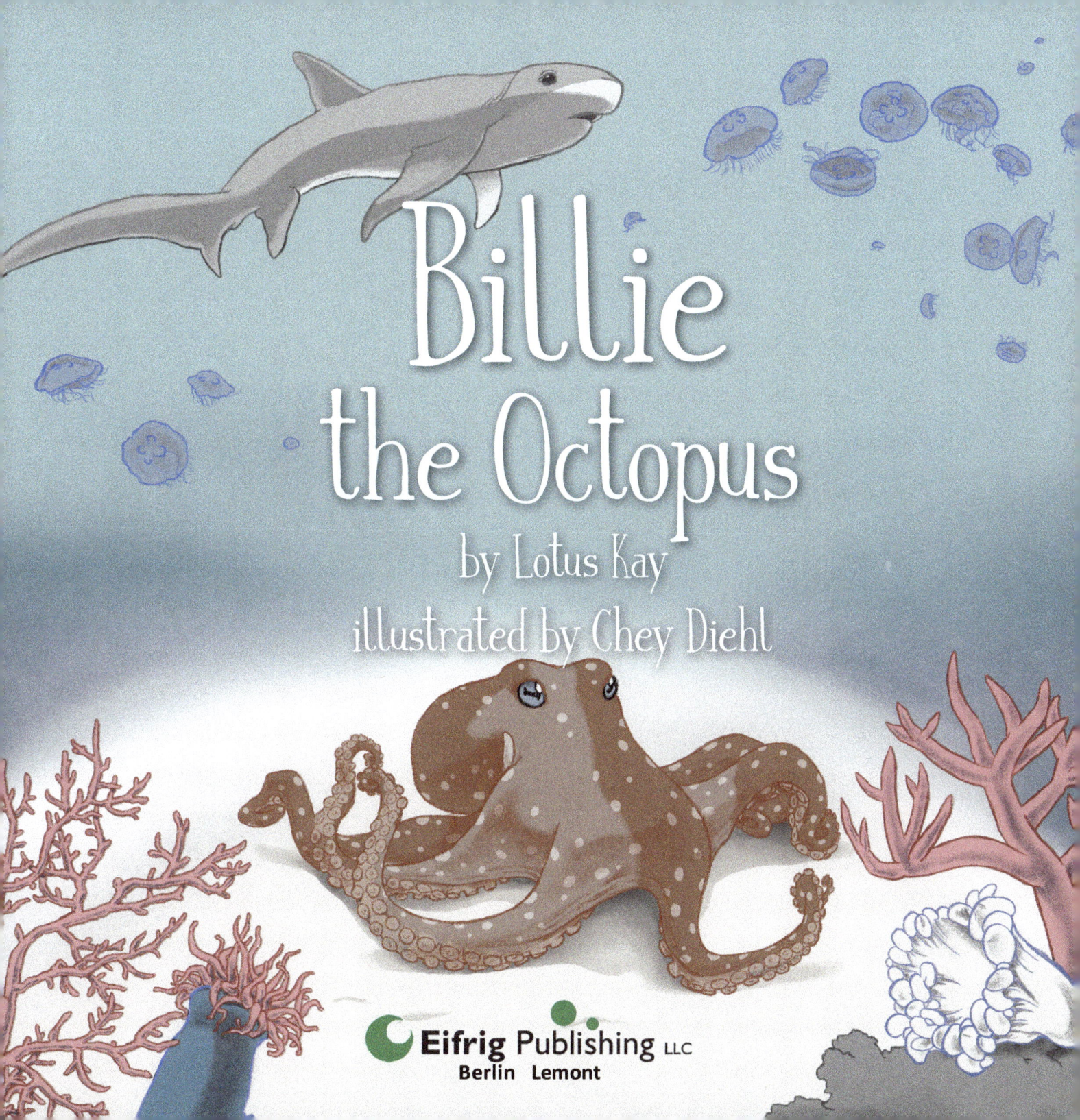

And inside this world
Many animals live in
You may have heard of them as "fishes"
You may have never met one face to face
But some people have on a dinner plate
But these creatures are worth a whole
Lot more than how they taste

So why don't we take a deeper look
Into the mind of Billie the octopus
Billie really wants you to know
All about her beautiful home

Now can't you see
All of the blue?
Without the ocean
There wouldn't be a me or you

Legend has it that's where all life began
And eventually we learned how to live on land
Fish learned how to crawl
And made their way onto the sand
And now here we are
Now we have legs to stand

You may have never met one face to face
But you may have seen some in an aquarium tank
But these fishes like to swim long distances
Not stay in one place

They want to enjoy their lives just like us
And why spread around harm
When you could spread around love?

Now let's take another look
Into the mind of Billie the octopus.
She wants you to know the truth
That if we keep taking from the ocean
That won't be very wise to do

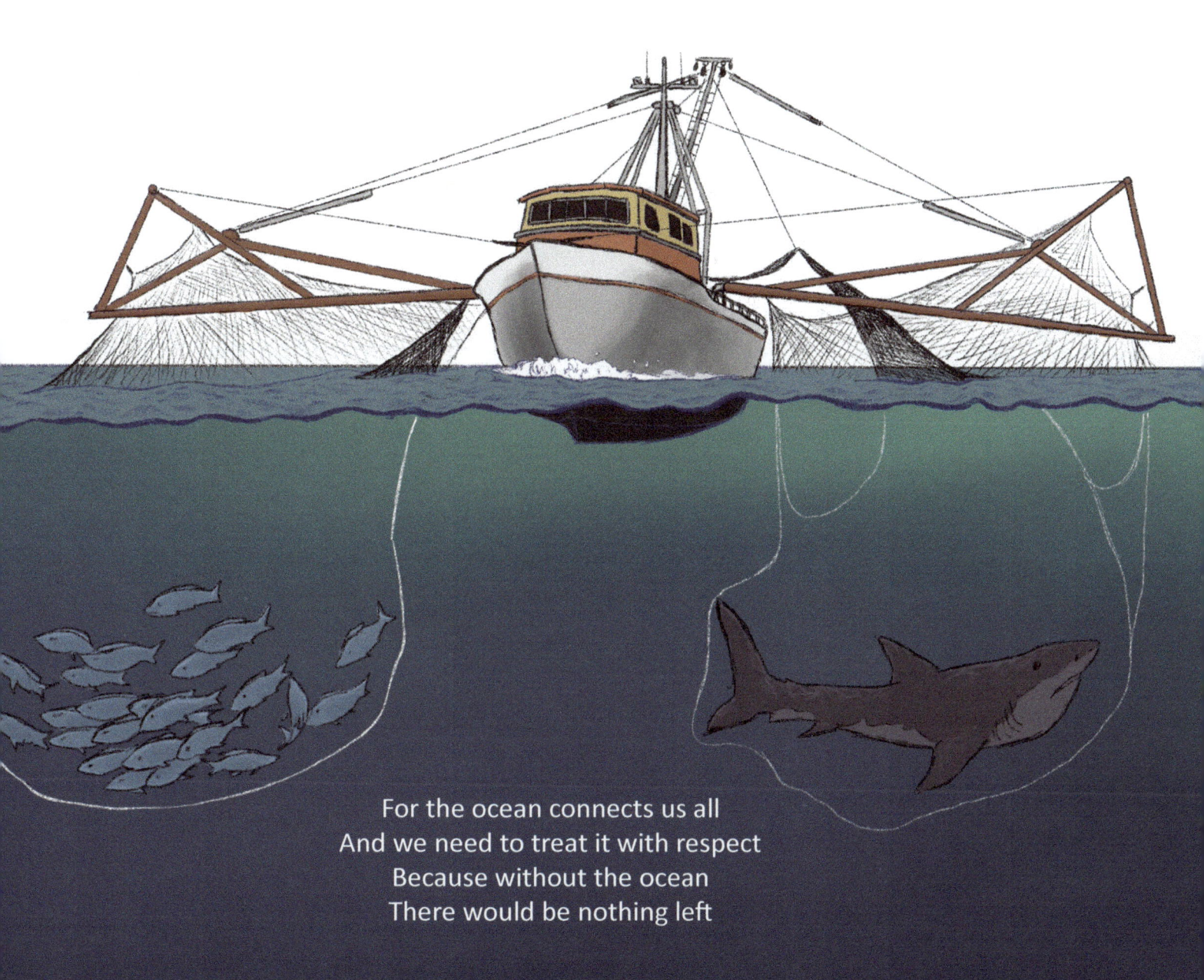

For the ocean connects us all
And we need to treat it with respect
Because without the ocean
There would be nothing left

Ocean Facts:

The ocean provides life for **97 percent** of the Earth's livable habitat and is home to more than **700,000 species**.[1]

Around **70 percent** of the Earth's surface is covered by ocean.[2]

About **70 percent** of the oxygen we breathe is produced by marine life in the ocean. There's oxygen from ocean plants in every breath we take.[2]

Unfortunately, in just **55 years** humans have managed to wipe out **90 percent** of the ocean's top predators. These include sharks, bluefin tuna, swordfish, marlin, and king mackerel.[3]

You may have heard people claim sharks are scary, but actually, sharks are only the cause of about **10 human deaths per year** while humans are the cause of about **11,417 shark deaths per hour**.[4]

Around **73 million** sharks are thrown back into the ocean each year with their fins cut off.[5]

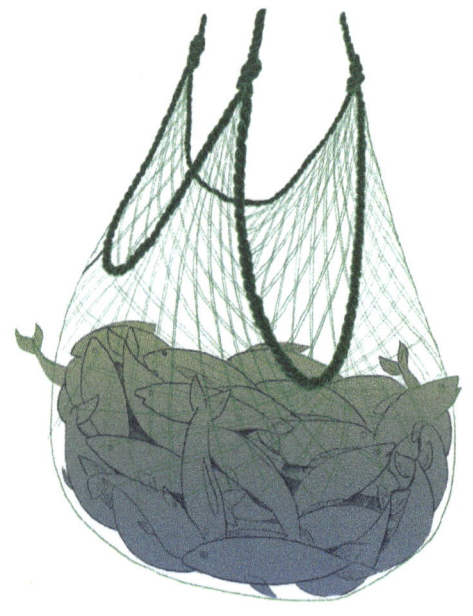

Sharks are definitely not the only species affected by fishing. All ocean life is affected by fishing. Even the ones we don't eat. **308,000** whales, dolphins, and porpoises die each year after becoming entangled in fishing equipment.[6]

It's estimated that for every 1 pound of shrimp on your dinner table, 26 pounds of other sea creatures were killed and tossed back into the sea, such as sea turtles. More than **50,000** sea turtles get caught in fishing nets meant to catch shrimp every year.[7]

The fishing of wild salmon impacts **137** species. Turtles, rays, dolphins, sharks, and endangered albatross often get caught when fishing for tuna. Beyond just fish, sea birds also get caught in fishing gear.[8]

Longlines with baited hooks can extend up to **50 miles**. These unintentionally attract and kill a huge range of sea mammals.[9]

New research shows that industrial fisheries are responsible for dumping nearly **10 million tons** of perfectly good fish back into the ocean each year—enough to fill 4,500 Olympic-sized swimming pools.[10]

Research has shown fish feel pain and stress with a central nervous system like humans. Even fish that are caught and thrown back into the water usually experience suffocation, sickness and internal injuries that often result in death.[11]

Fish live in water that is so polluted, that when you eat seafood you're ingesting this toxic brew—bacteria, contaminants, heavy metals, and much more.[12]

Confining fish or marine mammals at aquariums or marine parks in small tanks that restrict their movement for human entertainment can cause them harm. Fish and other aquatic animals which would swim many miles a day in the wild, are typically confined in small spaces and suffer from stress, deficient diets, disease, and a cramped and unbalanced environment. Wild orcas and dolphins, for example, usually live in large social groups and swim vast distances in the ocean. In captivity, these animals can only swim in endless circles in their tanks and are denied the opportunity to engage in any natural behavior.[13]

Keeping fish in fish tanks at home isn't good for them either: many of them are doomed to live in plastic bags or tiny glass bowls, neither of which provides the space or oxygen that goldfish need.[14]

SOURCES: 1: greenpeace.org; 2: nationalgeographic.com; 3: onegreenplanet.org; 4: greenpeace.org; 5: hakaimagazine.com; 6: worldwildlife.org 7: treehugger.com / oceana.org; 8: wildsalmoncenter.org 9: seafoodwatch.org; 10: gizmodo.com; 11: smithsonianmag.com; 12: peta.org; 13: peta.org; 14: peta.org

Visit **www.tinyurl.com/oceanfacts** for full sources and additional information about our oceans!

Plastic Facts:

Right now it is estimated that up to **12 million metric tons** of plastic—everything from plastic bottles and bags to microbeads—ends up in our oceans each year.[1]

Only **9 percent** of all plastic is recycled, **12 percent is burned**, and **79 percent** is in landfills and our oceans.[2]

Enough plastic is thrown away each year to circle the Earth four times.[3]

A study predicted there could be **more plastic than fish** by 2050.[4]

Around the world, an estimated **one million birds** and **100,000 marine mammals and sea turtles** die each year when they become trapped in plastic or eat it mistaking it for food. It is one of the biggest threats to all whales and dolphins occurring throughout the world's oceans.[5]

Something like an apple will start to turn brown and decompose and eventually see its last day, like most things in nature, while there's plastic from **100 years ago** still around today. Plastic doesn't biodegrade, which means once it's made, it can take many years to disappear. Some plastic never does.[6]

8 million tons of plastic enters our ocean from the land each year.[7]

The USA uses an average of **2,500,000** plastic bottles every hour.[8]

1 million sea birds die every year from plastic pollution.[9]

Plastic items can take up to **1000 years** to decompose in landfills. Plastic bags we use in our everyday life take 10-1000 years to decompose, while plastic bottles can take 450 years or more. Americans only recycle **0.6 percent of the 100 billion plastic bags** they take home from stores every year; the rest end up in landfills or as litter.[10]

Globally humans buy **a million plastic bottles per minute**—91 percent of which are not recycled.[11]

Climate change due to human activity has led to record-breaking rapid warming of the Earth's oceans over the past few decades. This warming has contributed to rising sea levels, ocean acidification, the destruction of coral reefs and marine life, and declining ocean oxygen levels.[12]

Now let's take another look
Into the mind of Billie the Octopus
You are just the person she's been wanting to tell
About what's going on to her home
Because she knows that you can help!

- When grocery shopping, ask your parents to come with their own reusable bag to put groceries in instead of walking out with a plastic one.

- Instead of using plastic water bottles, get a reusable one.

- Don't use plastic straws.

- When you do use plastic, always put it in the recycling bin instead of the garbage.

- Don't eat seafood and don't go fishing!

- Don't support aquariums or marine parks, and don't buy a fish as a pet. If you already have a pet fish at home, find out ways to make life for your fish better.

- Find out about organizations doing good things and how you can support them.

- Urge your elected officials to protect and defend our oceans.

- Educate your family and friends about what you learned in this book.

SOURCES: 1: greenpeace.org; 2: nationalgeographic.com; 3: ecowatch.com; 4: businessinsider.com; 5: wdcs.org; 6: livescience.com; 7: oceanconservancy.org; 8: byui.edu; 9: oceancrusaders.org; 10: business-ethics.com; 11: forbes.com; 12: science.sciencemag.org

Visit **www.tinyurl.com/plasticfacts** for full sources and additional information about plastic!

MORE BEAUTIFUL THAN HEAVEN AND *BILLIE THE OCTOPUS*

Written by Lotus Kay / Illustrated by Chey Diehl

These books have companion stuffed toys of their main characters and are attached to an educational campaign called **Bears for Cares**. The project is connected to the **Jane Goodall Institute**'s youth program **Roots & Shoots** and delivers a powerful message to foster awareness and change in young people.

Lotus wrote **More Beautiful Than Heaven** to raise awareness about the beauty of nature and the Earth, the endangered state of wildlife and our environment, and ultimately inspire children to care for and protect the planet and our fellow inhabitants. She then wrote **Billie the Octopus** to educate kids about the beauty and importance of the ocean and protecting fish and marine life.

Both books have stuffed animals that are characters in the book that can be found at the **Bears for Cares** website: "Beary" (the polar bear in **More Beautiful Than Heaven**) and "Billie" (the octopus), which support the Roots & Shoots program.

For more information on the **Bears for Cares** campaign or to purchase the stuffed toys that accompany this book, visit www.bearsforcares.com.

These books are printed in the USA on recycled, acid-free paper.

A portion of the proceeds from both books will be donated to the **Jane Goodall Institute** and its **Roots & Shoots** program.

In 2016, author Lotus Kay and her sister Jazmin received a grant from Jane Goodall's youth education program **Roots & Shoots** for their idea called **Bears for Cares**. The goal of their project was to help children around the world understand the state of wildlife and endangered species by gifting stuffed animals and educational children's books. The sisters teamed up with environmentally-friendly company Hugg-a-Planet to make the stuffed animals, which are also available with a stuffed Earth to educate kids about the planet.

www.rootsandshoots.org

Founded in 1991 by legendary primatologist Dr. Jane Goodall, Jane Goodall's **Roots & Shoots** is a youth service program for young people of all ages. **Roots & Shoots**' mission is to foster respect and compassion for all living things, to promote understanding of all cultures and beliefs, and to inspire each individual to take action to make the world a better place for people, other animals, and the environment.

The Jane Goodall Institute promotes understanding and protection of great apes and their habitat and builds on the legacy of Dr. Jane Goodall to inspire individual action by young people of all ages to help animals, other people and to protect the world we all share.

Find out more at www.janegoodall.org.

About the Author: Lotus Kay

Lotus Kay is a teen writer. Her writings have been published in various publications such as *Thrive Global, Vegan Health & Fitness Magazine, New Leaves, Light of Consciousness,* and *Voya: Voice of Youth Advocates*. She is a recipient of a grant from Jane Goodall's *Roots and Shoots* program for her work creating an educational campaign called *Bears for Cares* to educate youth about endangered species and wildlife. She is the author of **More Beautiful Than Heaven** and **Billie the Octopus**, both in collaboration with *Bears for Cares*, to educate kids on the importance and beauty of nature, and motivate them to help protect the Earth.

About Bears for Cares:

On Endangered Species Day, Lotus Kay and her sister Jazmin teamed up with *Hugg-A-Planet* to launch the new *Bears for Cares* foundling collection of stuffed animals to raise awareness for their generation on the state of wildlife and endangered species worldwide. *Bears for Cares* donates a portion of its proceeds to the Jane Goodall Institute and her *Roots & Shoots* program, while also being a sweet and meaningful gift made out of eco-friendly materials.
For more information, visit www.bearsforcares.com.

About the Artist: Chey Diehl

Chey Diehl is an illustrator who started drawing by copying pictures of anime in kindergarten. For a long time anime heavily influenced her style until she was able to attend her dream school, Savannah College of Art and Design, and develop her own style. She graduated Summa Cum Laude in June 2016 with a Bachelor of Fine Arts in Illustration. Currently, Chey is an active member of the Society of Children's Book Writers & Illustrators. Check out www.CheyDiehl.com for her portfolio.

www.ingramcontent.com/pod-product-compliance
Lightning Source LLC
Chambersburg PA
CBHW040013080526
44586CB00028B/2991